The Exalted Mahāyāna Sūtra on the
Wisdom Gone Beyond called

The Vajra Cutter

based on the
Tibetan Lhasa Zhol printing

translated into English by
Gelong Thubten Tsultrim
(American Buddhist monk George Churinoff)

FPMT Inc.
1632 SE 11th Avenue
Portland, OR 97214 USA
www.fpmt.org

© George Churinoff, 2002, 2007
All rights reserved.

No part of this book may be reproduced in any form or by any means, electronic or mechanical, including photocopying, recording, or by any information storage and retrieval system or technologies now known or developed, without permission in writing from the publisher.

Set in Microsoft Phagspa

Printed in the USA.

The Vajra Cutter Sūtra

In the language of India:
Ārya Vajracchedikā Nāma Prajñāpāramitā Mahāyāna Sūtra[1]

In Tibetan:
'Phags pa shes rab kyi pha rol tu phyin pa rdo rje
gcod pa zhes bya ba theg pa chen po'i mdo

In English:
The Exalted Mahāyāna Sūtra on the
Wisdom Gone Beyond called *The Vajra[2] Cutter*

I prostrate to all the buddhas and bodhisattvas.

Thus did I hear at one time. The Bhagavān was dwelling at Śrāvastī, in the grove of Prince Jeta, in the garden of Anāthapiṇḍada,[3] together with a great Sangha of bhikṣhus of 1,250 bhikṣhus and a great many bodhisattva mahāsattvas.

Then, in the morning, having put on the lower and upper Dharma robes and carried the begging bowl, the Bhagavān entered the great city of Śrāvastī to request alms. Then, having gone to the great city of Śrāvastī to request alms, the Bhagavān afterwards enjoyed the alms food, and having performed the activity of food,[4] since he had given up alms of later food,[5] put away the begging bowl and upper robe. He washed his feet, sat upon the prepared cushion, and having assumed the cross-legged posture, straightened the body upright and placed mindfulness in front. Then, many bhikṣhus approached to the place where the Bhagavān was and, having reached there, bowing their heads to the Bhagavān's feet, circumambulated three times and sat to one side.

Also at that time, the venerable Subhūti, joining that very assembly, sat down. Then, the venerable Subhūti rose from the seat, placed the upper robe over one shoulder, set his right knee on the ground, bowed, joining the palms, toward the Bhagavān, and said this to the Bhagavān: "Bhagavān, the extent to which the Tathāgata Arhat Perfectly Enlightened Buddha has benefited the bodhisattva mahāsattvas with highest benefit, the extent to which the Tathāgata has entrusted the bodhisattva mahāsattvas with highest entrustment – Bhagavān, it is astonishing; Sugata,[6] it is astonishing. Bhagavān, how should one who has correctly entered the bodhisattva's vehicle abide, how practice, how control the mind?"

That was said, and the Bhagavān said to the venerable Subhūti, "Subhūti, well said, well said. Subhūti, it is so; it is so. The Tathāgata has benefited the bodhisattva mahāsattvas with the highest benefit. The Tathāgata has entrusted the bodhisattva mahāsattvas with the highest entrustment. Subhūti, therefore, listen and properly retain it in mind, and I will explain to you how one who has correctly entered the bodhisattva's vehicle should abide, how practice, how control the mind."

Having replied, "Bhagavān, so be it," the venerable Subhūti listened in accordance with the Bhagavān, and the Bhagavān said this: "Subhūti, here, one who has correctly entered the bodhisattva's vehicle should generate the mind [of enlightenment] thinking this: 'As many as are included in the category of sentient being – born from egg, born from the womb, born from heat and moisture, born miraculously; with form, without form, with discrimination, without discrimination, without discrimination but not without [subtle] discrimination – the realm of sentient beings, as many as are designated by imputation as sentient beings, all those I shall cause to pass completely beyond sorrow into the realm of nirvana without remainder of the aggregates. Although limitless sentient beings have thus been caused to pass completely beyond sorrow, no sentient being whatsoever has been caused to pass completely beyond sorrow.'

"Why is that? Subhūti, because if a bodhisattva engages in discriminating a sentient being, he is not to be called a 'bodhisattva.' Why is that? Subhūti, if anyone engages in discriminating a sentient being, or engages in discriminating a living being, or engages in discriminating a person, they are not to be called a 'bodhisattva.'

"Further, Subhūti, a bodhisattva gives a gift without abiding in a thing; gives a gift without abiding in any phenomenon whatsoever. A gift should be given not abiding in visual form; a gift should be given not abiding in sound, smell, taste, tactility, or phenomenon either. Subhūti, without abiding in discriminating anything whatsoever as any sign, thus does a bodhisattva give a gift. Why is that? Subhūti, because the heap of merit of that bodhisattva who gives a gift without abiding, Subhūti, is not easy to take the measure of.

"Subhūti, what do you think about this? Do you think it is easy to take the measure of space in the east?"

Subhūti replied, "Bhagavān, it is not so."

The Bhagavān said, "Subhūti, similarly, do you think it is easy to take the measure of space in the south, west, north, above, below, the intermediate directions, and the ten directions?"

Subhūti replied, "Bhagavān, it is not so."

The Bhagavān said, "Subhūti, similarly, the heap of merit of that bodhisattva who gives a gift without abiding is also not easy to take the measure of.

"Subhūti, what do you think about this? Is one viewed as the Tathāgata due to the perfect marks?"[7]

Subhūti replied, "Bhagavān, it is not so; one is not viewed as the Tathāgata due to the perfect marks. Why is that? Because, that itself which the Tathāgata called perfect marks are not perfect marks."

He replied thus, and the Bhagavān said this to the venerable Subhūti: "Subhūti, to the degree there are perfect marks, to that degree there is deception. To the degree there are no perfect marks,[8] to that degree there is no deception. Thus, view the Tathāgata as marks and no marks."[9]

He said that and the venerable Subhūti replied to the Bhagavān, "Bhagavān, in the future period, at the end of the five hundred,[10] when the holy Dharma will totally perish, will any sentient beings produce correct discrimination upon the words of sūtras[11] such as this[12] being explained?"

The Bhagavān said, "Subhūti, do not say what you have said, '...in the future period, at the end of the five hundred, when the holy Dharma will totally perish, will any sentient beings produce correct discrimination upon the words of sūtras such as this being explained...'[13] Moreover, Subhūti, in the future period, at the end of the five hundred, when the holy Dharma will totally perish, there will be bodhisattva mahāsattvas, endowed with morality, endowed with qualities, endowed with wisdom. Subhūti, those bodhisattva mahāsattvas moreover will not have made homage to just a single buddha; they will not have produced roots of virtue to just a single buddha. Subhūti, there will be bodhisattva mahāsattvas who have made homage to many hundred thousands of buddhas and produced roots of virtue to many hundred thousands of buddhas.

"Subhūti, those who will acquire merely a single mind of faith upon the words of such sūtras as this being explained, Subhūti, the Tathāgata knows. Subhūti, they are seen by the Tathāgata; Subhūti, all those sentient beings will produce and perfectly collect an unfathomable heap of merit. Why is that? Subhūti, because those bodhisattva mahāsattvas will not engage in discriminating a self and will not discriminate a sentient being, will not discriminate a living being, will not engage in discriminating a person.

"Subhūti, those bodhisattva mahāsattvas will not engage in discriminating phenomena nor discriminating non-phenomena; nor will they engage in discrimination or non-discrimination.[14] Why is that? Subhūti, because if those bodhisattva mahāsattvas engage in discriminating phenomena, that itself would be of them[15] grasping a self and grasping a sentient being, grasping a living being, grasping a person. Because even if they engage in discriminating phenomena as non-existent,[16] that would be of them grasping a self and grasping a sentient being, grasping a living being, grasping a person.

"Why is that? Further, Subhūti, because a bodhisattva should not wrongly grasp phenomena, nor grasp non-phenomena."

Therefore, thinking of that, the Tathāgata said, "If, by those who know this Dharma treatise as like a boat, even dharmas should be given up, what need is there to mention non-dharmas?"[17]

Further, the Bhagavān said to the venerable Subhūti, "Subhūti, what do you think about this? Does that dharma that was manifestly and completely realized by the Tathāgata, unsurpassed perfect and complete enlightenment, exist whatsoever? Has any Dharma been taught by the Tathāgata?"[18]

He said that, and the venerable Subhūti replied to the Bhagavān, "Bhagavān, as I understand this meaning that was taught by the Bhagavān, that dharma that was manifestly and completely realized by the Tathāgata, unsurpassed perfect and complete enlightenment, does not exist whatsoever. That dharma that was taught by the Tathāgata does not exist whatsoever. Why is that? Because any dharma manifestly and completely realized or taught by the Tathāgata is not to be grasped, not to be expressed; it is not dharma nor is it non-dharma. Why is that? Because ārya beings are differentiated[19] by the uncompounded."[20]

The Bhagavān said to the venerable Subhūti, "Subhūti, what do you think about this? If some son of the lineage or daughter of the lineage, completely filling this billionfold world system[21] with the seven types of precious things, were to give gifts,[22] do you think that son of the lineage or daughter of the lineage would produce an immense heap of merit on that basis?"

Subhūti replied, "Bhagavān, immense. Sugata, immense. That son of the lineage or daughter of the lineage would produce an immense heap of merit on that basis. Why is that? Bhagavān, because that very heap of merit is not a heap; therefore, the Tathāgata says, 'Heap of merit, heap of merit.'"

The Bhagavān said, "Subhūti, compared to any son of the lineage or daughter of the lineage who, completely filling this billionfold world system with the seven types of precious things, were to give gifts, if someone, having taken[23] even as little as one stanza of four lines from this discourse of Dharma, also were to explain and correctly and thoroughly teach it to others, on that basis, the heap of merit produced would be much greater, incalculable, unfathomable.

Why is that? Subhūti, because the unsurpassed perfectly completed enlightenment of the tathāgata arhat perfectly completed buddhas arises from it; the buddha bhagavāns also are produced from it. Why is that? Subhūti, because the buddha dharmas called 'buddha dharmas,' are those buddha dharmas taught by the Tathāgata as non-existent; therefore, they are called 'buddha dharmas.'

"Subhūti, what do you think about this? Does the stream-enterer think, 'I have attained the result of stream-enterer'?"

Subhūti replied, "Bhagavān, it is not so. Why is that? Bhagavān, because one does not enter into anything whatsoever; therefore, one is called 'stream-enterer.' One has not entered into form, nor entered into sound, nor into smell, nor into taste, nor into tactility, nor entered into a phenomenon;[24] therefore, one is called 'stream-enterer.' Bhagavān, if that stream-enterer were to think 'I have attained the result of stream-enterer,' that itself would be a grasping of that as a self,[25] grasping as a sentient being, grasping as a living being, grasping as a person."

The Bhagavān said, "Subhūti, what do you think about this? Does the once-returner think, 'I have attained the result of once-returner'?"

Subhūti replied, "Bhagavān, it is not so. Why is that? Because the phenomenon of entry into the state of the once-returner does not exist whatsoever. Therefore, one says, 'once-returner.'"[26]

The Bhagavān said, "Subhūti, what do you think about this? Does the non-returner think, 'I have attained the result of non-returner'?"

Subhūti replied, "Bhagavān, it is not so. Why is that? Because the phenomenon of entry into the state of the non-returner does not exist whatsoever. Therefore, one says, 'non-returner.'"[27]

The Bhagavān said, "Subhūti, what do you think about this? Does the arhat think, 'I have attained the result of arhatship'?"

Subhūti replied, "Bhagavān, it is not so. Why is that? Because the phenomenon called 'arhat' does not exist whatsoever. Bhagavān, if the arhat were to think, 'I have attained the result of arhatship,' that itself would be a grasping of that as a self, grasping as a sentient being, grasping as a living being, grasping as a person.

"Bhagavān, I was declared by the Tathāgata Arhat Perfectly Completed Buddha as the foremost of those who abide without afflictions.[28] Bhagavān, I am an arhat, free of attachment; but, Bhagavān, I do not think, 'I am an arhat.' Bhagavān, if I were to think, 'I have attained arhatship,' the Tathāgata would not have made the prediction about me saying, 'The son of the lineage, Subhūti, is the foremost of those who abide without afflictions. Since not abiding in anything whatsoever, he abides without affliction, he abides without affliction.'"

The Bhagavān said, "Subhūti, what do you think about this? Does that dharma that was received by the Tathāgata from the Tathāgata Arhat Perfectly Completed Buddha Dīpaṇkara exist whatsoever?"

Subhūti replied, "Bhagavān, it is not so. That dharma that was received by the Tathāgata from the Tathāgata Arhat Perfectly Completed Buddha Dīpaṇkara does not exist whatsoever."

The Bhagavān said, "Subhūti, if some bodhisattva were to say, 'I shall actualize arranged fields,'[29] they would speak untruly. Why is that? Subhūti, because arranged fields called 'arranged fields,' those arrangements are taught by the Tathāgata as non-existent; therefore, they are called 'arranged fields.' Subhūti, therefore, the bodhisattva mahāsattva thus should generate the mind without abiding, should generate the mind not abiding in anything. They should generate the mind not abiding in form, should generate the mind not abiding in sound, smell, taste, tactility, or phenomenon.

"Subhūti, it is like this: If, for example, the body of a being were to become thus, were to become like this, as big as Sumeru, the king of mountains, Subhūti, what do you think about this? Would that body[30] be big?"

Subhūti replied, "Bhagavān, that body would be big. Sugata, that body would be big. Why is that? Because it is taught by the Tathāgata as not being a thing; therefore, it is called a 'body.' Since it is taught by the Tathāgata as not being a thing; therefore, it is called a 'big body.'"

The Bhagavān said, "Subhūti, what do you think about this? If there were also just as many Ganges Rivers as there are grains of sand in the river Ganges, would their grains of sand be many?"

Subhūti replied, "Bhagavān, if those very Ganges Rivers were many, there is no need to mention their grains of sand."

The Bhagavān said, "Subhūti, you should appreciate; you should understand.[31] If some man or woman, completely filling with the seven kinds of precious things that many world systems as there are grains of sand of those rivers Ganges,[32] were to offer that to the tathāgata arhat perfectly completed buddhas, Subhūti, what do you think about this? Would that man or woman produce much merit on that basis?"

Subhūti replied, "Bhagavān, much. Sugata, much. That man or woman would produce much merit on that basis."

The Bhagavān said, "Subhūti, compared to someone who, completely filling that many world systems with the seven types of precious things, were to give gifts to the tathāgata arhat perfectly completed buddhas, if someone, having taken even as little as a stanza of four lines from this discourse of Dharma, were to explain it and correctly and thoroughly teach it also to others, on that basis the merit that itself would produce would be much greater, incalculable, unfathomable.

"Furthermore, Subhūti, if, at whatever place on earth even a stanza of four lines from this discourse on Dharma is recited or taught, that place on earth is a real shrine[33] of the world with devas, humans, and asuras, what need to mention that whoever takes up this discourse of Dharma, memorizes, reads, understands, and properly takes to mind[34] will be most astonishing. At that place on earth [where] the Teacher resides; other levels of gurus also abide."[35]

He said that and the venerable Subhūti replied to the Bhagavān, "Bhagavān, what is the name of this discourse of Dharma? How should it be remembered?"

He said that and the Bhagavān replied to the venerable Subhūti, "Subhūti, the name of this Dharma discourse is the 'wisdom gone beyond'; it should be remembered like that. Why is that? Subhūti, because the very same wisdom gone beyond that is taught by the Tathāgata is not gone beyond; therefore, it is called 'wisdom gone beyond.'

"Subhūti, what do you think about this? Does the dharma that is taught by the Tathāgata exist whatsoever?"

Subhūti replied, "Bhagavān, the dharma that is taught by the Tathāgata does not exist whatsoever."[36]

The Bhagavān said, "Subhūti, what do think about this? Are the quantities of particles of earth that exist in a billionfold world system many?"

Subhūti replied, "Bhagavān, the particles of earth are many. Sugata, they are many. Why is that? Bhagavān, because that which is a particle of earth was taught by the Tathāgata as not being a particle; therefore, it is called 'particle of earth.' That which is a world system was taught by the Tathāgata as not being a world system; therefore, it is called a 'world system.'"

The Bhagavan said, "Subhūti, what do you think about this? Is one to be viewed as the Tathāgata Arhat Perfectly Completed Buddha due to those thirty-two marks of a great being?"

Subhūti replied, "Bhagavān, it is not so. Why is that? Bhagavān, because those thirty-two marks of a great being that are taught by the Tathāgata are taught by the Tathāgata as no marks; therefore, they are called 'thirty-two marks of the Tathāgata.'"[37]

The Bhagavān said, "Further, Subhūti, compared with some man or woman completely giving up bodies numbering the grains of sand of the river Ganges, if someone, taking even as little as a stanza of four lines from this discourse of Dharma, also were to teach it to others,[38] they would produce on that basis many greater merits, incalculable, unfathomable."

Thereupon, the venerable Subhūti, due to the impact of the Dharma, shed tears. Having wiped away the tears, he replied to the Bhagavān, "Bhagavān, this discourse on Dharma taught thus by the Tathāgata,[39] Bhagavān, is astonishing. Sugata, it is astonishing. Bhagavān, since my production of exalted wisdom, I have never before heard this discourse on Dharma. Bhagavān, those sentient beings who will produce correct discrimination upon this sūtra being explained will be most astonishing. Why is that? Bhagavān, because that which is correct discrimination is not discrimination; therefore, correct discrimination was taught by the Tathāgata saying 'correct discrimination.' Bhagavān, upon this Dharma discourse being explained, that I imagine and appreciate is not astonishing[40] to me. Bhagavān, in the final time, in the final age, at the end of the five hundred, those sentient beings who take up this Dharma discourse, memorize, read, and understand it will be most astonishing. Furthermore, Bhagavān, they will not engage in discriminating a self; will not engage in discriminating a sentient being, discriminating a living being, discriminating a person. Why is that? Bhagavān, because that itself which is discrimination as a self, discrimination as a sentient being, discrimination as a living being, and discrimination as a person is not discrimination. Why is that? Because the buddha bhagavāns are free of all discrimination."

He said that and the Bhagavān replied to the venerable Subhūti, "Subhūti, it is so; it is so. Upon this sūtra being explained, those sentient beings who are unafraid, unterrified, and will not become terrified will be most astonishing. Why is that? Subhūti, because this highest wisdom gone beyond, taught by the Tathāgata, the highest wisdom gone beyond that is taught by the Tathāgata, was also taught by unfathomable buddha bhagavāns – therefore, it is called 'highest wisdom gone beyond.'

"Further, Subhūti, that itself which is the patience gone beyond of the Tathāgata has not gone beyond. Why is that? Subhūti, because when the king of Kaliûga[41] cut off my limbs and appendages, at that time there did not arise in me discrimination as a self, discrimination as a sentient being, discrimination as a living being, nor discrimination as a person, and in me there was no discrimination whatsoever, yet there was also no non-discrimination. Why is that? Subhūti, because, if at that time there had arisen in me discrimination as a self, at that time there would also have arisen discrimination of malice; if there had arisen discrimination as a sentient being, discrimination as a living being, discrimination as a person, at that time there would also have arisen discrimination of malice.

"Subhūti, I know with clairvoyance that in the past period, during five hundred lifetimes, I was the rishi[42] called 'Preacher of Patience'; even then there did not arise in me the discrimination as a self; there did not arise the discrimination as a sentient being, discrimination as a living being, discrimination as a person. Subhūti, therefore, the bodhisattva mahāsattva, completely abandoning all discrimination, should generate the mind for unsurpassed perfectly complete enlightenment. One should generate the mind not abiding in form. One should generate the mind not abiding in sound, smell, taste, tactility, or phenomena. One should generate the mind not abiding in non-phenomena either. One should generate the mind not abiding in anything whatsoever. Why is that? Because that itself which is abiding does not abide. Therefore, the Tathāgata taught, 'The bodhisattva should give gifts not abiding.'

"Further, Subhūti, the bodhisattva should thus totally give away gifts for the welfare of all sentient beings. However, that itself which is discrimination as a sentient being is non-discrimination. Those themselves who were taught by the Tathāgata saying 'all sentient beings' also do not exist. Why is that? Subhūti, because the Tathāgata teaches reality, teaches truth, teaches what is; the Tathāgata teaches what is without error.

"Further, Subhūti, the dharma that is manifestly and completely realized or shown by the Tathāgata has neither truth nor falsity. Subhūti, it is like this, for example: if a man with eyes has entered darkness, he does not see anything whatsoever; likewise should one view the bodhisattva who totally gives up a gift by falling into anything.

"Subhūti, it is like this, for example: upon dawn and the sun rising, a man with eyes sees various kinds of forms; likewise should one view the bodhisattva who totally gives up a gift by not falling into anything.

"Further, Subhūti, those sons of the lineage or daughters of the lineage who take up this Dharma discourse, memorize, read, understand, and correctly and thoroughly teach it to others in detail are known by the Tathāgata, they are seen by the Tathāgata. All those sentient beings will produce an unfathomable heap of merit.

"Further, Subhūti, compared to some man or woman, at the time of dawn, totally giving up bodies numbering the grains of sand of the river Ganges – also totally giving up bodies numbering the grains of sand of the river Ganges at the time of midday and evening, in such number totally giving up bodies for many hundred thousands of ten million, hundred billion eons[43] – if someone, having heard this Dharma discourse, would not reject it, if they themselves would produce much greater merit on that basis, incalculable, unfathomable, what need to mention someone who, having written it in letters, takes it up, memorizes, reads, understands, and correctly and thoroughly teaches it to others in detail?

"Further, Subhūti, this Dharma discourse is unimaginable and incomparable.[44] This Dharma discourse was taught by the Tathāgata for the benefit of sentient beings who have correctly entered into the supreme vehicle, the welfare of sentient beings who have correctly entered into the best vehicle. Those who take up this Dharma discourse, memorize, read, understand, and correctly and thoroughly teach it to others in detail are known by the Tathāgata; they are seen by the Tathāgata. All those sentient beings will be endowed with an unfathomable heap of merit. Being endowed with an unimaginable heap of merit, incomparable, immeasurable, and limitless, all those sentient beings will hold my enlightenment on the shoulder. Why is that? Subhūti, this Dharma discourse is unable to be heard by those who appreciate the inferior, by those viewing a self, by those viewing a sentient being, by those viewing a living being; those viewing a person are unable to hear, to take up, to memorize, to read, and to understand because that cannot be.

"Further, Subhūti, at whatever place on earth this sūtra is taught, that place on earth will become worthy to be paid homage by the world with devas, humans, and asuras. That place on earth will become worthy as an object of prostration and worthy as an object of circumambulation. That place on earth will become like a shrine.⁴⁵

"Subhūti, whatever son of the lineage or daughter of the lineage takes up the words of a sūtra like this, memorizes, reads, and understands, they will be tormented; will be intensely tormented.⁴⁶ Why is that? Subhūti, because whatever non-virtuous actions of former lifetimes that were committed by those sentient beings that would bring rebirth in the lower realms, due to torment in this very life, those non-virtuous actions of former lifetimes will be purified, and they will also attain the enlightenment of a buddha.

"Subhūti, I know with clairvoyance that in the past period, in even more countless of countless eons, much beyond even beyond⁴⁷ the Tathāgata Arhat Perfectly Completed Buddha Dīpaṅkara, there were eighty-four hundred thousands of ten million, hundred billion buddhas whom I pleased, and having pleased, did not upset. Subhūti, from whatever I did, having pleased and not having upset those buddha bhagavāns and in the future period, at the end of the five hundred, from someone taking up this sūtra, memorizing, reading, and understanding, Subhūti, compared to this heap of merit, the former heap of merit does not approach⁴⁸ even a hundredth part, a thousandth part, a hundred-thousandth part; does not withstand enumeration, measure, calculation, similarity, equivalence, or comparison.

"Subhūti, at that time, the sons of the lineage or daughters of the lineage will receive a quantity of heap of merit that, if I were to express the heap of merit of those sons of the lineage or daughters of the lineage, sentient beings would go mad, would be disturbed.

"Further, Subhūti, this Dharma discourse being unimaginable, its maturation indeed should also be known as unimaginable."

Then, the venerable Subhūti replied to the Bhagavān, "Bhagavān, how should one who has correctly entered the bodhisattva's vehicle abide, how practice, how control the mind?"

The Bhagavān said, "Subhūti, here, one who has correctly entered the bodhisattva's vehicle should generate the mind thinking this: 'I shall cause all sentient beings to pass completely beyond sorrow into the realm of nirvana without remainder of the aggregates. Although sentient beings were caused to pass completely beyond sorrow like that, no sentient being whatsoever was caused to pass beyond sorrow.' Why is that? Subhūti, because if a bodhisattva engages in discriminating a sentient being, he is not to be called a 'bodhisattva.' Also, if he engages in discriminating a person, he is not to be called a 'bodhisattva.' Why is that? Subhūti, because the dharma called 'one who has correctly entered the bodhisattva's vehicle' does not exist whatsoever.

"Subhūti, what do you think about this? Does that dharma that was manifestly and completely realized by the Tathāgata from the Tathāgata Dīpaṇkara, unsurpassed perfect and complete enlightenment, exist whatsoever?"

He said that and the venerable Subhūti replied to the Bhagavān, "Bhagavān, that dharma that was manifestly and completely realized by the Tathāgata from the Tathāgata Dīpaṇkara, unsurpassed perfect and complete enlightenment, does not exist whatsoever."

He said that and the Bhagavān replied to the venerable Subhūti, "Subhūti, it is so. It is so, that dharma that was manifestly and completely realized by the Tathāgata from the Tathāgata Dīpaṇkara, unsurpassed perfect and complete enlightenment, does not exist whatsoever. Subhūti, if that dharma that was manifestly and completely realized by the Tathāgata were to exist at all, the Tathāgata Dīpaṅkara would not have made the prediction to me, saying, 'Young brahmin, in a future period you will become the Tathāgata Arhat Perfectly Completed Buddha called Śākyamuni.' Subhūti, thus, since that dharma that was manifestly and completely realized by the Tathāgata, unsurpassed perfect and complete enlightenment, does not exist whatsoever, therefore, the Tathāgata Dīpaṅkara made the prediction to me, saying, 'Young brahmin, in a future period you will become the Tathāgata Arhat Perfectly Completed Buddha called Śākyamuni.' Why is that? Because, Subhūti, 'Tathāgata' is an epithet of the suchness of reality.[49]

"Subhūti, if someone were to say, 'The Tathāgata Arhat Perfectly Completed Buddha manifestly and completely realized unsurpassed perfect and complete enlightenment,' they would speak wrongly. Why is that? Subhūti, because that dharma that was manifestly and completely realized by the Tathāgata, unsurpassed perfect and complete enlightenment, does not exist whatsoever. Subhūti, that dharma that was manifestly and completely realized[50] by the Tathāgata has neither truth nor falsity. Therefore, 'all dharmas are buddha dharmas' was taught by the Tathāgata. Subhūti, 'all dharmas', all those are non-dharmas. Therefore, it is said that 'all dharmas are buddha dharmas.' Subhūti, it is like this, for example: like a human endowed with a body[51] and the body became large."

The venerable Subhūti replied, "Bhagavān, that taught by the Tathāgata, 'a human endowed with a body and a large body,' is taught by the Tathāgata as not being a body. Therefore, 'endowed with a body and a large body' is said."

The Bhagavān said, "Subhūti, it is so; if some bodhisattva were to say, 'I shall cause sentient beings to completely pass beyond sorrow,' he should not be called 'bodhisattva.' Why is that? Subhūti, does the dharma that is called 'bodhisattva' exist whatsoever?"

Subhūti replied, "Bhagavān, it does not."

The Bhagavān said, "Subhūti, therefore, it was taught by the Tathāgata that 'all dharmas are without a sentient being, without a living being, without a person.'

"Subhūti, if some bodhisattva were to say, 'I shall actualize arranged fields,' he too should be expressed similarly.[52] Why is that? Subhūti, because the arranged fields called 'arranged fields' are those taught by the Tathāgata as non-arranged. Therefore, they are called 'arranged fields.' Subhūti, whatever bodhisattva appreciates that dharmas are selfless, saying 'dharmas are selfless,' he is expressed by the Tathāgata Arhat Perfectly Completed Buddha as a bodhisattva called a 'bodhisattva.'[53]

"Subhūti, What do you think about this? Does the Tathāgata possess the flesh eye?"

Subhūti replied, "Bhagavān, it is so; the Tathāgata possesses the flesh eye."

The Bhagavān said, "Subhūti, what do you think about this? Does the Tathāgata possess the divine eye?"

Subhūti replied, "Bhagavān, it is so; the Tathāgata possesses the divine eye."

The Bhagavān said, "Subhūti, what do you think about this? Does the Tathāgata possess the wisdom eye?"

Subhūti replied, "Bhagavān, it is so; the Tathāgata possesses the wisdom eye."

The Bhagavan said, "Subhūti, what do you think about this? Does the Tathāgata possess the dharma eye?"

Subhūti replied, "Bhagavān, it is so; the Tathāgata possesses the dharma eye."

The Bhagavan said, "Subhūti, what do you think about this? Does the Tathāgata possess the buddha eye?"

Subhūti replied, "Bhagavān, it is so; the Tathāgata possesses the buddha eye."

The Bhagavān said, "Subhūti, what do you think about this? If, there being also just as many Ganges Rivers as there are grains of sand in the river Ganges, there were just as many world systems as there are grains of sand of those, would those world systems be many?"

Subhūti replied, "Bhagavān, it is so; those world systems would be many."

The Bhagavān said, "Subhūti, as many sentient beings as exist in those world systems, I totally know their continua of consciousness of different thoughts.[54] Why is that? Subhūti, because a so-called 'continuum of consciousness' is that taught by the Tathāgata as a non-continuum. Therefore, it is called a 'continuum of consciousness.' Why is that? Subhūti, because past consciousness does not exist as an observable, nor does future consciousness exist as an observable, nor does present consciousness exist as an observable.

"Subhūti, what do you think about this? If someone, completely filling this billionfold world system with the seven types of precious things, were to give gifts, do you think that son of the lineage or daughter of the lineage would produce an enormous heap of merit on that basis?"

Subhūti replied, "Bhagavān, enormous. Sugata, enormous."

The Bhagavān said, "Subhūti, it is so. It is so; that son of the lineage or daughter of the lineage would produce an enormous heap of merit on that basis. Subhūti, if a heap of merit were a heap of merit, the Tathāgata would not have taught a heap of merit called a 'heap of merit.'

"Subhūti, what do you think about this? Should one be viewed as the Tathāgata due to total achievement of the form body?"

Subhūti replied, "Bhagavān, it is not so; one should not be viewed as the Tathāgata due to total achievement of the form body. Why is that? Bhagavān, because 'total achievement of the form body' is that taught by the Tathāgata as not being total achievement; therefore, it is called 'total achievement of the form body.'"

The Bhagavān said, "Subhūti, what do you think about this? Is one to be viewed as the Tathāgata due to perfect marks?"

Subhūti replied, "Bhagavān, it is not so; one is not to be viewed as the Tathāgata due to perfect marks. Why is that? Because that which was taught by the Tathāgata as perfect marks was taught by the Tathāgata as not being perfect marks; therefore, they are called 'perfect marks.'"

The Bhagavān said, "Subhūti, what do you think about this? If it is thought that the Tathāgata considers, 'the dharma is demonstrated by me,' Subhūti, do not view it like that, because the dharma that is demonstrated by the Tathāgata does not exist whatsoever. Subhūti, if someone were to say 'the dharma is demonstrated by the Tathāgata,' Subhūti, he would deprecate me since nonexistent and wrongly seized. Why is that? Subhūti, because that demonstrated dharma called 'demonstrated dharma,' which is referred to saying 'demonstrated dharma,' does not exist whatsoever."

Then, the venerable Subhūti said to the Bhagavān, "Bhagavān, in the future period, will there be any sentient beings who, having heard this demonstration[55] of such a dharma as this, will clearly believe?"

The Bhagavān said, "Subhūti, they are not sentient beings nor non-sentient beings. Why is that? Subhūti, so-called 'sentient beings,' because they were taught by the Tathāgata as non-sentient beings, therefore are called 'sentient beings.'

"Subhūti, what do you think about this? Does that dharma that was manifestly and completely realized by the Tathāgata, unsurpassed perfect and complete enlightenment, exist whatsoever?"

The venerable Subhūti replied, "Bhagavān, that dharma that was manifestly and completely realized by the Tathāgata, unsurpassed perfect and complete enlightenment, does not exist whatsoever."

The Bhagavān said, "Subhūti, it is so; it is so. For it,[56] even the least dharma does not exist and is not observed;[57] therefore, it is called 'unsurpassed perfect and complete enlightenment.'

"Further, Subhūti, that dharma is equivalent since, for it, inequivalence[58] does not exist whatsoever; therefore, it is called 'unsurpassed perfect and complete enlightenment.' That unsurpassed perfect and complete enlightenment – equivalent as selfless, without sentient being, without living being, without person – is manifestly and completely realized through all virtuous dharmas. Subhūti, virtuous dharmas called 'virtuous dharmas,' they, taught by the Tathāgata as just non-dharmas, are therefore called 'virtuous dharmas.'

"Further, Subhūti, compared to any son of the lineage or daughter of the lineage collecting a heap of the seven types of precious things about equaling whatever Sumeru, king of mountains, exist in a billion world systems, and giving gifts, if someone, having taken up even as little as a stanza of four lines from this wisdom gone beyond, were to teach it to others, Subhūti, compared to this heap of merit, the former heap of merit having not approached even a hundredth part, does not withstand comparison.

"Subhūti, what do you think about this? If it is thought that the Tathāgata considers, 'Sentient beings are liberated by me,' Subhūti, do not view it like that. Why is that? Subhūti, because those sentient beings who are liberated by the Tathāgata do not exist whatsoever. Subhūti, if some sentient being were to be liberated by the Tathāgata, that itself would be, of the Tathāgata, grasping a self, grasping a sentient being, grasping a living being, grasping a person. Subhūti, so-called 'grasping a self,' that is taught by the Tathāgata as non-grasping, yet that is grasped by childish ordinary beings. Subhūti, so-called 'childish ordinary beings,' they were taught by the Tathāgata as just non-beings; therefore, they are called 'childish ordinary beings.'

"Subhūti, what do you think about this? Is one to be viewed as the Tathāgata due to perfect marks?"

Subhūti replied, "Bhagavān, it is not so; one is not viewed as the Tathāgata due to perfect marks."

The Bhagavān said, "Subhūti, it is so; it is so. One is not viewed as the Tathāgata due to perfect marks. Subhūti, if one were viewed as the Tathāgata due to perfect marks, even a chakravartin king would be the Tathāgata; therefore, one is not viewed as the Tathāgata due to perfect marks."

Then, the venerable Subhūti said to the Bhagavān, "Bhagavān, as I understand the meaning of what the Bhagavān has said, one is not viewed as the Tathāgata due to perfect marks."

Then, these verses were spoken by the Bhagavān at that time:

"Whoever sees me as form, whoever knows me as sound, has wrongly engaged by abandoning,[59] those beings do not see me.

The buddhas are dharmatā[60] viewed; the guides are the dharmakāya.
Since dharmatā is not to be known, it is unable to be known."[61]

"Subhūti, what do you think about this? If one grasps that 'the Tathāgata Arhat Perfectly Completed Buddha is due to perfect marks,' Subhūti, you should not view so for, Subhūti, the Tathāgata Arhat Perfectly Completed Buddha does not manifestly and completely realize unsurpassed perfect and complete enlightenment due to perfect marks.

"Subhūti, if one grasps that 'some dharma has been designated as destroyed or annihilated[62] by those who have correctly entered the bodhisattva's vehicle,' Subhūti, it should not be viewed so; those who have correctly entered the bodhisattva's vehicle have not designated any dharma whatsoever as destroyed or annihilated.

"Further, Subhūti, compared to any son of the lineage or daughter of the lineage who, completely filling with the seven kinds of precious things as many world systems as there are grains of sand of the rivers Ganges, were to give gifts, if any bodhisattva attained forbearance that dharmas are selfless and unproduced,[63] on that basis the heap of merit they themselves would produce would be much greater. Further, Subhūti, a heap of merit should not be acquired by the bodhisattva."

The venerable Subhūti replied, "Bhagavān, should not a heap of merit be acquired by the bodhisattva?"

The Bhagavān said, "Subhūti, acquire, not wrongly grasp;[64] therefore, it is called 'acquire.'

"Subhūti, if someone says, 'The Tathāgata goes or comes or stands or sits or lies down,' he does not understand the meaning explained by me. Why is that? Subhūti, because 'the Tathāgata' ('the One Gone Thus') does not go anywhere nor has come from anywhere; therefore, one says, 'the Tathāgata Arhat Perfectly Completed Buddha.'

"Further, Subhūti, if some son of the lineage or daughter of the lineage were to render as many atoms of earth as exist in a billionfold world system, like this for example, into powder like a collection of subtlest atoms, Subhūti, what do you think about this? Would that collection of subtlest atoms be many?"

Subhūti replied, "Bhagavān, it is so. That collection of subtlest atoms would be many. Why is that? Bhagavān, because if there were a collection, the Bhagavān would not have said 'collection of subtlest atoms.' Why is that? Because that 'collection of subtlest atoms' that was taught by the Bhagavān was taught by the Tathāgata as no collection; therefore, one says 'collection of subtlest atoms.' That 'billionfold world system' that was taught by the Tathāgata was taught by the Tathāgata as no system; therefore, one says 'billionfold world system.' Why is that? Bhagavān, because if there were to be a world system, that itself would be grasping a solid thing. That taught by the Tathāgata as grasping a solid thing was taught by the Tathāgata as no grasping; therefore, one says 'grasping a solid thing.'"

The Bhagavān said, "Subhūti, grasping a solid thing is itself a convention; that dharma does not exist as expressed, yet it is grasped by ordinary childish beings. Subhūti, if someone were to say, 'Viewing as a self was taught by the Tathāgata and viewing as a sentient being, viewing as a living being, viewing as a person was taught by the Tathāgata,' Subhūti, would that be spoken by right speech?"

Subhūti replied, "Bhagavān, it would not. Sugata, it would not. Why is that? Bhagavān, because that which was taught by the Tathāgata as viewing as a self, was taught by the Tathāgata as no viewing; therefore, one says, 'viewing as a self.'"

The Bhagavān said, "Subhūti, those who have correctly entered the bodhisattva's vehicle should know, should view, should appreciate all dharmas like this; they should appreciate[65] like this, not abiding whatsoever in any discrimination as a dharma. Why is that? Subhūti, because discrimination as a dharma, called 'discrimination as a dharma,' is taught by the Tathāgata as non-discrimination; therefore, one says 'discrimination as a dharma.'

"Further, Subhūti, compared to any bodhisattva mahāsattva who, completely filling unfathomable and incalculable world systems with the seven kinds of precious things, were to give gifts, if any son of the lineage or daughter of the lineage who, having taken[66] as little as a stanza of four lines from this perfection of wisdom, were to memorize or read or understand or correctly and thoroughly teach it to others in detail, on that basis the merit he himself would produce would be more, incalculable, unfathomable.

"How should one correctly and thoroughly teach? Just how one would not correctly and thoroughly teach; therefore, one says, 'correctly and thoroughly teach.'

"As a star, a visual aberration, a lamp, an illusion, dew, a bubble, a dream, lightning, and a cloud – view all the compounded like that."

That having been said by the Bhagavān, the elder[67] Subhūti, those bodhisattvas,[68] the fourfold disciples – bhikshus, bhikshunis, upāsakas and upāsikas[69] – and the world with devas, humans, asuras, and gandharvas, overjoyed, highly praised that taught by the Bhagavān.

The Exalted Mahāyāna Sūtra on the Wisdom Gone Beyond called *The Vajra Cutter* is concluded.

Colophon to the Lhasa Zhol text: [70]
Compiled, revising the translation of the Indian abbot Śilendra Bodhi and Yeshe sDe with the new language standard.

Colophon to the English translation:
This translation of the Vajra Cutter Sūtra is based on the Tibetan Lhasa Zhol text, having compared it with various other Tibetan printings as well as with Sanskrit versions, and having viewed several excellent earlier English translations. It was completed on 22 March 2002 at the Chandrakirti Tibetan Buddhist Meditation Centre, near Nelson, New Zealand, by Gelong Thubten Tsultrim (the American Buddhist monk George Churinoff).

First revised edition including minor revisions by the translator, June 2007.

Bibliography

The Vajra Cutter Sūtra, from the Lhasa Zhol bKa'-'gyur, shes phyin sna tshogs, vol. ka, folios 215a–235b, originally printed in 1934.

The Vajra Cutter Sūtra, from the Tog Palace Manuscript of the Tibetan Kanjur, vol. 51, Leh, 1979.

The Vajra Cutter Sūtra, small edition republished by FPMT (details unknown)

Lanchou edition of the *Vajra Cutter and Its Commentary* (rDo rje gcod pa dang de'i 'grel ba bzhugs so) containing the Vajra Cutter Sūtra with the commentary of Cone Gragspa.

Vajracchedikā Prajñāpāramitā, edited and translated by Edward Conze, Serie Orientale Roma, Istituto Italiano per il Medio ed Estremo Oriente, vol. 13, 1957.

"The Manuscript of the Vajracchedikā Found at Gilgit, An Annotated Transcription and Translation by Gregory Schopen, 1989." In Studies in the Literature of the Great Vehicle: Three Mahāyāna Buddhist Texts, edited by L. O. Gómez and J. A. Silk. Ann Arbor: The University of Michigan, pp. 89–139.

Extensive Commentary of the Exalted Vajra Cutter Wisdom Gone Beyond ('Phags pa shes rab kyi pha rol tu phyin pa rdo rje gcod pa'i rgya cher 'grel pa), by Kamalaâhīla, translated by the team Mañjuârī, Jinamitra, and Yeshe sDe, from volume mDo 'grel ma of the sDe dge bstan 'gyur, TOH 3818, mDo 'grel ma 204a–67a.

Materials for a Dictionary of the Prajñāpāramitā Literature, Edward Conze, Suzuki Research Foundation, Tokyo, 1973.

The Practical Sanskrit-English Dictionary, Vaman Shivaram Apte, Rinsen Book Co., Kyoto, 1992.

Tibetan-Sanskrit Dictionary, Lokesh Chandra, Rinsen Book Co., Kyoto, 1982.

Notes

1. The words of the title of the sūtra have a slightly different order in the various editions.
2. Often translated as *Diamond Sūtra* or *Diamond Cutter Sūtra*. However, the word "vajra" used in the title is not explained as meaning "diamond" in either the sūtra itself or the Indian commentaries we have access to (those of Asaûga, Vasu-bandhu, and Kamalaâhīla). In fact, the Buddha does not even mention the word "vajra" in the discourse itself (at least not in the Tibetan or Sanskrit editions), naming it merely "Prajñāparamitā": "Subhūti, the name of this Dharma discourse is 'the wisdom gone beyond'; it should be remembered like that."

    In his introduction to his edition and translation, the Buddhist scholar Edward Conze said (p. 7): "It is usual, following Max Mueller, to render Vajracchedikā Sūtra as <<Diamond Sutra>>. There is no reason to discontinue this popular usage, but strictly speaking, it is more than unlikely that the Buddhists here understand vajra as the material substance which we call 'diamond.'"

    Kamalaâhīla's commentary (p. 204a) takes "vajra" to mean the adamantine implement: "Like this, it is the 'vajra cutter' in two ways. Because it cuts off the afflicted obstructions and the subtle obstructions to omniscience, which are as difficult to destroy as the vajra – this indicates the necessity to abandon the two obstructions. Alternatively, the cutting is 'vajra-like' since it is similar to the shape of the vajra: the vajra is made bulbous on the ends and thin in the center. Similarly, this wisdom gone beyond is also taught as extensive in the beginning and the end – the ground of aspirational activity and the buddha ground. The thin middle indicates the pure grounds of superior intention. Hence, it is like

the aspect of a vajra, and this indicates three grounds as its subject matter."
3. The name of one of Buddha's principal lay sponsors often appears in Pali as Anāthapiṇḍika.
4. Kamalaâhīla's commentary (pp. 6b-7) explains that "the activity of food" includes many aspects of the activity, all done to benefit sentient beings in some way.
5. Kamalaâhīla's commentary (p. 7b) explains this as referring to the special ascetic virtues prescribed by Buddha (Sanskrit: dūta-guṇgāë; Tibetan: sbyangs pa'i yon tan), which include eating only once during the day.
6. Literally, "One who has Gone to Bliss" (Skt: sugata; Tib: bde bar gsheg pa), which is a common epithet of the Buddha.
7. "Due to perfect marks" (Skt: lakṣana-sampadā; Tib: mtsan phun sum tsogs pas) can be translated from Sanskrit as "due to possessing marks"; the word sampad meaning "achieve-ment," "possession," etc. Hence, Conze's choice of "possession of his marks." However, sampad also means "perfection," "excellence," etc. (Apte, p. 1,644), and it is this meaning used in Kamalaâhīla's commentary (p. 220b): "Since situated in position, clear and complete, they are also perfect..." (Tib: de dag kyang yul na gnas pa dang, gsal ba dang, rdzogs pas phun sum tsogs pa'o).
8. Read "'di ji snyam du sems, mtsam phun sum tsogs pa" as "ji tsam du mtsan phun sum tsogs pa," in accordance with the Tog Palace, small and Lanchou editions.
9. Conze and others take "lakṣana-alakṣaṇatas tathāgato draṣåavyaë" as "the Tathāgata is to be seen from no-marks as marks." (The Sacred Books of the East edition has on p. 115: "lakṣaṇālakṣaṇatvataë.") However, the Tibetan translations have: "de bzhin gshegs pa la mtsan dang mtsan ma med par blta'o" (reading our text's

"mtsan dang mtsan med" as the other texts read "mtsan dang mtsan ma med"), which takes the compound "lakṣaṇa-alakṣaṇa" as "marks and no marks" instead of "no-marks as marks."

The Tibetan translation accords with Kamalaâhīla's commentary (p. 221a): "'...To the degree there are perfect marks' means 'ultimately, to the degree there is adherence to the perfect marks, to that degree there is wrong adherence.' 'To the degree there are no perfect marks' is to be understood as explained oppositely. This indicates here how one should practice – by equipoise in yoga. Here is indicated how to guard the mind – through abandoning the two extremes. 'Thus' one should view the Tathāgata due to marks, like the magically created Buddha. This dispels the extreme of deprecation, because of not deprecating the nirmāṇakāya of the Bhagavān conventionally. No marks are to be viewed ultimately, because marks are not established at all. This dispels the extreme of superimposition."

10. Kamalaâhīla's commentary explains this (on p. 220a): "Since the doctrine of the Bhagavān is famed "to remain until five sets of five hundred...,' therefore, 'the end' is treated in particular because of the preponderance of the five dregs at that time."
11. The Lhasa Zhol and Tog Palace editions have "bshad pa 'di la," which I find hard to understand, whereas our other two editions have "bshad pa dag la," or "upon explanations," which accords with Kamalaâhīla (p. 221b) and the Sanskrit.
12. Kamalaâhīla (p. 221b) "...'such as this' means profound and extensive meaning..."
13. All four Tibetan editions have the Bhagavān telling Subhūti not to make the statement that is quoted, whereas the Sanskrit can be read, as Conze does, to

have the Bhagavān say, "Do not speak thus Subhūti!" and then to say, "Yes, there will be in the future period..." This seems to be more in accord with the following word "moreover" in the Lhasa Zhol and Tog Palace editions.
14. Since the Tog Palace and Lanchou editions accord with the Sanskrit as well as with Kamalaâhīla's commentary (p. 223a), we have translated that here. The Lhasa Zhol edition has: "...nor will they engage in discriminating as discrimination or non-discrimination"; the small text has: "...nor will they engage in non-discrimination."
15. The small text has "by them"; the other three have "of them." Conze translates the Sanskrit "tesām" as "with them" – thus, "...that would be with them a seizing on a self..."
16. This entire sentence is lacking in the Sanskrit. However, it occurs in one of three variations in the Tibetan editions. The Lhasa Zhol edition has "...even if they engage phenomena as non-existent..."; the Tog Palace edition has "...even if they engage in discriminating phenomena as non-existent..."; the Lanchou and small texts have "...even if they engage in discriminating phenomena as selfless..." Kamalaâhīla's commentary does not mention it, leaving one to assume it may not have appeared in the version he was using.

17. As the next sentence begins by again introducing the Bhagavān as the speaker, it is unclear whether the Bhagavān made this statement on this occasion. Kamalaâhīla's commentary (p. 224b) quotes the Ārya Ratna Karaṇḍaka Sūtra ('Phags pa dkon mchog za ma tog gi mdo): "Reverend Subhūti, if, by those who know the Dharma treatise as like a boat, even dharmatā should be given up, what need is there to mention non-

dharmas? Nor is the abandoning of any dharma even non-dharma."
18. The Lanchou and small texts both have "...realized by the Tathāgata as unsurpassed..." and "Has that Dharma been taught at all..."
19. Kamalaâhīla's commentary (p. 225b) quotes a text (which he calls Compendium of Buddha, (Tib: Sangs rgyas yang dag par sdud pa), Buddha-saægīti: "Ānanda, that which is the non-production, the non-disintegration, the non-abiding, and the non-alteration of phenomena is 'the ārya truth.' Ānanda, the Tathāgata having considered this, said, 'The ārya hearers (ârāvaka) are distinguished by the uncompounded.' This (means) whether the tathāgatas arise or do not arise, because of permanently existing like that and unchangeable, (they are) uncompounded. Because of realizing that, the ārya beings are distinguished by that because the āryas are distinguished by realizing the uniqueness of phenomena (chos kyi de kho na). Because another unique entity is unsuitable."
20. Read "'dus ma byas" for "'dus ma bgyis." Perhaps the intention of the editor of the Lhasa Zhol text here is to make "uncompounded" more honorific, as it refers to that which distinguishes the ārya beings.
21. Literally, "the great thousand of three thousand world systems" (Skt: trisāhasramahāsāhasram lokadhātu; Tib: stong gsum gyi stong chen po'i 'jig rten gyi khams), which is well known in Buddhist literature. Here, the basic world referred to includes four continents, the sun and moon, Sumeru (king of mountains), the desire realm gods, and the first of the form realms of Brahma.

The "world systems of three thousand" refers to the three categories of such worlds – a thousand basic world systems (with the four continents, etc.) called "the

small thousand," a thousand of those (or a million such world systems) called "the middling thousand," and a thousand of those (or a billion world systems) called "the great thousand." The last of the three categories, "the great thousand of three thousand world systems," thus includes a billion world systems.
22. No recipient is specified in any of the four Tibetan editions nor in Kamalaâhīla's commentary at this point, whereas Conze's Sanskrit edition specifies the recipients as the tathāgata arhat perfectly completed buddhas.
23. Kamalaâhīla's commentary (p. 227a) explains "having taken" as "done in recitation" (bzung nas ni zhes bya ba kha ton du byas ba'o). The Tibetan commentary says (p. 93-4), "To take is to take the words to mind – suitable to apply even to having the text in hand – and to recite."
24. The Lhasa Zhol and Tog Palace editions both have singular. The Lanchou and small texts both have plural.
25. Conze translates the Sanskrit (section 9a) "sa eva tasya-ātma-grāho bhavet sattva-grāho jīva-grāho pudgala-grāho bhaved iti" as "...then that would be in him a seizing of self, seizing of a being, seizing of a soul, seizing of a person." However, the Tibetan commentary explains the genitive "of that" ("de'i" or "de yi") as follows (p. 95): "Saying, 'that itself would be grasping of that as a self' (de nyid de yi bdag tu 'dzin par 'gyur ro) teaches (grasping to) the person and the result as self-grasping and true grasping. The first is grasping to a self of the person and the second is grasping to a self of phenomena."

One might argue that it is better to translate the phrase "de nyid de'i bdag tu 'dzin par 'gyur lags so" as, "that itself would be a grasping to a self of that," rather than, "that itself would be a grasping of that as a self." But, according to the Prāsaûgika Madhyamaka school, the mental action called "self-grasping" or "grasping as a self" (bdag tu 'dzin pa) takes as its referent object the conventional self (of a person or other phenomena) and conceives of it as a truly existent self. The "self" of "self-grasping" is not what is being grasped.

26. The Lhasa Zhol and Tog Palace editions, as well as the Sanskrit edition used by Conze, leave out the following sentence found in the other two Tibetan editions: "Bhagavān, if the once-returner were to think 'I have attained the result of once-returner,' that itself would be a grasping of that as a self, grasping as a sentient being, grasping as a living being, grasping as a person."

27. Again, the following sentence is left as before: "Bhagavān, if a non-returner were to think, 'I have attained the result of non-returner,' that itself would be a grasping of that as a self, grasping as sentient being, grasping as a living being, grasping as a person."

28. Conze translates this as "the foremost of those who dwell in peace" (Skt: araṇā-vihāriṇām agryo; Tib: nyon mongs pa med par gnas pa rnams kyi mchog). In the translation of The Middle Length Discourses of the Buddha (Majjhima Nikāya) (p. 1,345, n. 1,263), it is mentioned that Subhūti was recognized as foremost in two categories, "those who live without conflict and those who are worthy of gifts."

    Although the Sanskrit word "araṇa" can mean "not fighting" (Apte, p. 213) and hence, "without conflict" or "peace," the Tibetan translation of "nyon mongs pa med pa" as "without afflictions" might reflect the intention of this epithet, in that Subhūti was said to be very angry as a youth and had to overcome this faulty behavior in particular to achieve higher realizations.

29. Arranged fields (Skt: kṣetra-vyūhān; Tib: zhing bkod pa rnams) [translated by Conze as "harmonies of Buddha-

fields" and by Schopen as "'wonderful arrangements' in my sphere of activity"] refers to the bodhisattva activity of creating the causes of their future buddha-field.

30. Conze's Sanskrit edition has "personal existence" (Skt: ātmabhāva) at this point and in the following paragraph for the word "body" (Skt: kāya; Tib: lus). However the Sanskrit word kāya is used at the beginning of this paragraph (...if, for example, the body of a being were to become thus, were to become like this, as big as Sumeru...)

31. Conze's Sanskrit edition has "ārocayāmi te Subhūti prativedayāmi te," which he translates as "This is what I announce to you, Subhuti; this is what I make known to you" – both sentences in the first person. However, all four Tibetan editions used for this translation have "rab 'byor, khyod mos par bya, khyod kyis khong du chud par bya'o," the second phrase of which translates as "you should understand." The first phrase could be translated as "I shall announce to you" if we assume the Tibetan word "mos" ("appreciate" or "believe") is actually "smos" ("mention" or "announce"), one Sanskrit equivalent of "smos" being "ārocayati" (see Lokesh Chandra, p. 1,882).

    To complicate things further, Kamalaâhīla's commentary (p. 233a) has "mos par bya zhes bya ba ni 'dod pa ste, mos pa bskyed par bya'o khong du chud par bya'o zhes bya ba ni rtogs par bya ba ste shes rab bskyed do zhes bya ba'i tha tsig go / 'di la snga ma ni phyi ma'i 'bras bu'o / yang na phyi ma ni snga ma'i bshed pa'o / bshed ces bya ba ni sgra'o / wang dag par bstan zhes bya ba ni 'dod pa ste mos par bskyed pa'i don to."

32. The Lhasa Zhol edition differs from the other three Tibetan editions and Conze's Sanskrit edition by saying, "...world systems equal to the grains of sand of the river

Ganges." As this would seem to ignore the immediately previous elaborate example, the version of the other texts is used here on the assumption of scribal error.
33. "Real shrine" (Tib: mchod rten du gyur; Skt: caityabhūta).
34. The Lhasa Zhol and Tog Palace editions as well as Kamalaâhīla's commentary (p. 233b) agree on this list. The Lanchou and small editions have "whoever takes up this discourse of Dharma, writes, memorizes, holds, reads, understands, and properly takes to mind..."
35. The wording of the Lhasa Zhol and Tog Palace editions differs from that of the Lanchou and small editions. The former is as translated above (sa phyogs de na ston pa yang bzhugs te, bla ma'i gnas gzhan dag kyang gnas so); the later could be translated as "At that place on earth either the Teacher or some such guru abides (sa phyogs de na ston pa'm, bla ma lta bu gang yang rung bar gnas so).
36. The Gilgit fragment begins from this point.
37. The Lhasa Zhol and Tog Palace editions both have "thirty-two marks of the Tathāgata" where as the Lanchou, small, and Sanskrit editions have "thirty-two marks of a great being."
38. The Lanchou and small editions have "If someone, taking even as little as a stanza of four lines from this discourse of Dharma, were to correctly teach it to others..." The text of the Gilgit fragment for this paragraph accords with the Lhasa Zhol and Tog Palace editions.

Conze's translation, "The Lord: And again Subhuti, suppose a woman or man would day by day renounce all they have and all they are, as many times as there grains of sand in the river Ganges, and if they should renounce all they have and all they are for as many aeons as there are grains of sand in the river Ganges – but if someone else would, after taking from this discourse

on Dharma but one stanza of four lines, demonstrate and illuminate it to others...," mixes elements from other texts.
39. The wording of the Lanchou and small editions differs: "This discourse on Dharma taught however much by the Tathāgata..." Kamalaâhīla's commentary (p. 236b) accords with that reading and explains "however much" as meaning "explain to the bodhisattvas with however many ways as are worthy to be explained."
40. Although the Lhasa Zhol and Tog Palace editions have "appreciate" (Tib: mos pa), the other two Tibetan editions, Kamalaâhīla's commentary (p. 237b), as well as the Gilgit Sanskrit fragment all have "astonishing" (Tib: ngo mtshar; Skt: āâcaryaæ), and Conze's Sanskrit edition chooses "difficult" (Skt: duṣkaraæ).
41. Although Schopen notes the Gilgit fragment has "evil king" (Skt: kalirājaë), all four Tibetan editions as well as Conze's Sanskrit have "kaliûga."
42. Skt: öṣi.
43. Ten million (Skt: koåi; Tib: bye ba) and hundred billion (Skt: niyuta; Tib: khrag khrig) are commonly used in denoting large numbers.
44. Although missing in the Lhasa Zhol edition and Conze's Sanskrit edition, the Tog Palace, Lanchou, and small editions each have an additional phrase here, "One should understand as just unimaginable also the maturation of this."
45. Tib: mchod rten; Skt: caitya (caityabhūta). The Sanskrit word stupa is also translated as the same Tibetan word mchod rten but the Sanskrit text has caitya. Earlier in the text the phrase "mchod rten du gyur" was translated "real shrine." Here the Tibetan phrase "mchod rten lta bur 'gyur ro" is translated as "'will become like a shrine."

46. "Tormented" (Tib: mnar ba; Skt: paribhūta). The Sanskrit paribhūta is translated by Conze as "humbled" and by Schopen as "ridiculed." However, Apte (p. 982) defines paribhūta as "1. Overpowered, conquered. 2. Disregarded, slighted." The Tibetan mnar ba also refers to torture or excruciating pain in general. The Tibetan commentary by Cone Gragspa (pp. 119–20) lists "various illnesses and quarrels, disputes, unearthing of faults and bondage, beating, and so forth." Schopen notes (note 11, p. 137) "that unmeritorious karma could be eliminated as a result of being abused by others for having adopted a particular practice or position," but the general position seems to be that non-meritorious karma is purified by undergoing many types of suffering.
47. The Lhasa Zhol and Tog Palace editions have "beyond," which agrees with the Sanskrit. The small and Lanchou editions have "before."
48. Lhasa Zhol and Tog Palace editions have "mi pod"; the small and Lanchou editions have "nye bar mi 'gro." Both phrases can be translations of the Sanskrit nopaiti, "to approach."
49. Tib: yang dag pa de zhin nyid; Skt: bhūta-tathatāyā.
50. The Lhasa Zhol and Tog Palace editions as well as the Gilgit fragment have as here translated. The small and Lanchou editions as well as one of the several Sanskrit editions Conze consulted (that of Pargiter) have the additional phrase "or taught."
51. The small and Lanchou editions have "a being endowed with a human body."
52. "Similarly" here means "he should not be called a 'bodhisattva.'" See Schopen (n. 15, p. 138).
53. The Lhasa Zhol and Tog Palace editions and the Gilgit fragment have "bodhisattva" repeated twice. The small and Lanchou editions and Conze's Sanskrit edition have

"bodhisattva" followed by "mahāsattva."
54. "Different thoughts" (Skt: nānābhāvāæ; Tib: bsam pa tha dad pa) is translated by Conze as "manifold" and by Schopen as "various," but the Tibetan translation takes the Sanskrit bhāvāæ as "thoughts" or "inclinations" (Tib: bsam pa).
55. The other three Tibetan texts have "explanation" (Tib: bshad pa). In Schopen's "Textual Note about Folio 9b" (p. 117, note 6), he seems to reconstruct the Sanskrit of "explanation" [Skt: (bhāṣyamā)ṇāæ] and cites several editions that have a Sanskrit equivalent of "explanation." Conze leaves the verb out.
56. The Lhasa Zhol and Tog Palace texts have simply "it" (Tib: de) whereas the small and Lanchou texts have "for it" (or "there") (Tib: de la). Conze's edition and the Gilgit fragment have the Sanskrit tatra ("for it" or "there.")
57. The small and Lanchou texts have the opposite order, i.e., "is not observed and does not exist."
58. The small and Lanchou texts have "inequivalence and equivalence do not exist there," but Conze's Sanskrit edition and the Gilgit fragment have only "for it, inequivalence does not exist whatsoever" (Skt: na tatra kiæcid viṣamas).
59. The small and Lanchou texts have "have engaged in the wrong path" (Tib: log pa'i lam du zhugs pa ste) but the Lhasa Zhol and Tog Palace texts read "have wrongly engaged by abandoning" (Tib: log par spong bas zhugs pa ste), which agrees with the Sanskrit in Conze's edition and in the Gilgit fragment, "mithyā-prahāṇa-prasötā).
60. The Sanskrit word dharmatā (Tib: chos nyid) refers to the nature of dharmas, the nature of phenomena. Here, it refers to the ultimate nature of phenomena, not just the conventional nature nor the doctrine (as is translated by Conze and Schopen).

61. Cone Gragspa's Tibetan commentary (p. 141) says, "The reason of not seeing (in the first stanza) is that it is necessary to view the dharmakāya of the buddhas, the nature body, as the body of ultimate nature (dharmatā) – and the body of the guides, the buddhas, dharmatā, ultimate truth, is not an object to be known by an awareness bound by true grasping, because the dharmakāya is unable to be known by that awareness." See also the discussion in Kamalaâhīla's commentary (pp. 259a–b).
62. Skt: kasyacid dharmasya vināâaë prajñapta ucchedo va (veti); Tib: chos la la zhig rnam par bshig gam, chad par btags pa.
63. The Lhasa Zhol text has "selfless and unproduced" as does Conze's Sanskrit edition (nirātmakeṣv anutpattikeṣu). The Gilgit fragment has just "selfless" (nirātmakeṣu), leaving out "unproduced."
The small and Lanchou texts agree with the Lhasa Zhol edition as to "selfless and unproduced" but have (parenthetical material from the commentary of Cone Gragspa, p. 143) "...if any bodhisattva (directly realized the meaning of) selfless (in dependence on this) Dharma discourse (the wisdom gone beyond text) and attained (the great) forbearance about (the phenomena of) non-production..."
64. "Subhūti, acquire, not wrongly grasp" (Tib: rab 'byor, yongs su gzung mod kyi, log par mi gzung ste; Skt: parigrahītavyaë subhūte nograhītavyaë). The Sanskrit reads, "should be acquired, Subhūti, not should be grasped."
65. The small and Lanchou texts have "know" (Tib: shes).
66. Although the small and Lanchou texts have the word written (Tib: bris), the Lhasa Zhol and Tog Palace texts have taken (Tib: blang), which agrees with the Conze's Sanskrit edition and the Gilgit fragment (Skt: udgöhya).

Furthermore, Kamalaâhīla's commentary (p. 265b) explains taken (Tib: blang) as "reading in recitation" (Tib: blangs nas zhes bya ba ni kha ton du bklags pa'o).

67. "Elder" (Skt: sthavira; Tib: gnas brtan)
68. The three other Tibetan texts have "those bhikṣhus, those bodhisattvas..."
69. Upāsakas and upāsikas are lay men and women who have taken the life-long vows of a lay practitioner. Novice monks and novice nuns can be included in the categories of bhikṣhus and bhikṣhunis, the fully ordained monks and fully ordained nuns.
70. The colophon is found in the catalogue of the Lhasa Zhol edition of the collection of Tibetan translations of Buddha's Words (bka' 'gyur). The index of the ACIP says the Lhasa Zhol edition was composed in 1934 at the request of the Thirteenth Dalai Lama. The actual individual texts in the Lhasa Zhol edition, however, were translated at various times before that.
    The colophon says, in full, "From p. 215 front (till p. 235 back), the "Three Hundred Wisdom Gone Beyond" or "Vajra Cutter." One Section (bam bo). Compiled, revising the translation of the Indian abbot Śilendra Bodhi and Yeshe sDe with the new language standard."

Foundation for the Preservation of the Mahayana Tradition

The Foundation for the Preservation of the Mahayana Tradition (FPMT) is a dynamic worldwide organization devoted to education and public service. Established by Lama Thubten Yeshe and Lama Zopa Rinpoche, FPMT touches the lives of beings all over the world. In the early 1970s, young Westerners inspired by the intelligence and practicality of the Buddhist approach made contact with these lamas in Nepal and the organization was born. Now encompassing over 150 Dharma centers, projects, social services and publishing houses in thirty-three countries, we continue to bring the enlightened message of compassion, wisdom, and peace to the world.

We invite you to join us in our work to develop compassion around the world! Visit our web site at www.fpmt.org to find a center near you, a study program suited to your needs, practice materials, meditation supplies, sacred art, and online teachings. We offer a membership program with benefits such as Mandala magazine and discounts at the online Foundation Store. And check out some of the vast projects Lama Zopa Rinpoche has developed to preserve the Mahayana tradition and help end suffering in the world today. Lastly, never hesitate to contact us if we can be of service to you.

Foundation for the Preservation of the Mahayana Tradition
1632 SE 11th Avenue
Portland, OR 97214 USA
(503) 808-1588

www.fpmt.org

FPMT Education Services

Education Services at FPMT International Office offers a vast range of Buddhist study programs, prayer books, and practice materials from the Gelugpa lineage. Our study programs meet the needs of beginners through to the most advanced students, from courses introducing Buddhism to the study of Tibetan and the highest philosophical texts.

As the Dharma takes root outside of Tibet, we make clear translations of Buddhist texts, prayers, and teachings available through our study programs and publications. We work with translators around the world to provide texts in English, Spanish, Chinese, French, German, and many other languages.

Working in collaboration with the Lama Yeshe Wisdom Archive, we publish Buddhist prayer books, sadhanas, retreat materials, and practice texts, many with commentary by Lama Thubten Yeshe and Lama Zopa Rinpoche. We also offer DVDs and CDs of prayers and teachings that inspire and inform. Whatever your interest, FPMT Education Services provides the materials you need to actualize the Buddhist path.

Education Services
FPMT International Office
1632 SE 11th Avenue
Portland OR 97214
(503) 808-1588
education@fpmt.org

www.fpmt.org

Made in the USA
Las Vegas, NV
18 September 2023